# How To Conquer

# Strife

---

## KENNETH COPELAND

### KCP

Kenneth Copeland Publications
Fort Worth, Texas

**How to Conquer Strife**

ISBN 1-57562-103-7          30-0035

© 1987 Kenneth Copeland Publications

Reprinted 1997

All scripture is from the *King James Version*
unless otherwise noted.

Kenneth Copeland Publications
Fort Worth, Texas  76192-0001

# How to Conquer Strife

The fight is on—at every level. Strife is separating nation from nation, brother from sister and husband from wife. The conflict comes in varying degrees—from minor disagreements at the office to bomb-dropping border disputes between nations. But one thing is certain, if you're going to live in this world, you're going to have to deal with it! And, as a believer, you're going to have to deal with it severely.

Strife isn't something you can treat casually. It's a deadly enemy. Just look at what the Word says about it. James 3:16 says where strife is there is confusion and EVERY evil work. Allowing strife to go unchecked or entering into it opens the door to every evil work. Careful study of the New Testament reveals strife as a deadly enemy that must be stopped in our daily lives.

In fact, as a born-again child of God, you're not only expected to avoid strife, you're expected to be a "peacemaker" (Matthew 5:9). But is it really possible to live in a world that's so full of strife without being drawn into the conflict yourself?

That's a question I used to ask myself a lot. My life used to be full of turmoil and conflict. Even as a boy, I fought over everything—my bike, my clothes, anything. It seems like I was always fighting!

When I was in grade school I stood out like a sore thumb because all of the other boys wore bluejeans and I wore corduroy knickerbockers. So other boys made fun of me by imitating the sound my corduroy britches made as I walked, "Whoosh, whoosh, whoosh, whoosh." And all of the other kids laughed at me. That always started a fight!

It never took much provocation for me to end up in some kind of strife with someone. Even as an adult, I'd look for opportunities to fight. I'd try saying something ugly in the elevator and then watch all the women's ears roll up! Then I'd hope some fellow would say something about it so that maybe I'd get to hit him! I was pretty ornery before I made Jesus the Lord of my life.

Even after I was born again, I could be pretty ornery. But then I fought with my tongue instead of my fist. I said cutting things that packed a more powerful punch than my fist ever did. Instead of slugging a man in the face, I hit him in the heart and that was much more devastating. A black eye will heal in just a few days, but a wounded spirit will fester and fester until someone reaches in there with the love of God to heal it.

What I couldn't understand is why I spoke more harshly to my family than to anyone else. It seemed that no matter how hard I tried, I couldn't speak a kind word to them. I criticized Gloria's driving so much that she nearly refused to drive while I was with her. And I criticized her flying until she finally decided to just sleep and let old "bad mouth" do all the flying. The way I spoke to my children was no better.

I didn't want to be so insensitive, but I couldn't help it. I had a well-developed habit of speaking harshly and didn't know how to change it. One day I realized that I could hardly remember the last time I said something kind to my children. That was when I decided that I had to change some things. But how?

I asked the Lord, "How do I change a pattern of behavior that's been part of me for so long?" I knew that Ephesians 4:29 said, *"Let no corrupt communication proceed out of your mouth, but that which is good to the use of edifying, that it may minister grace unto the hearers."* And harsh words and criticism are certainly not edifying and gracious. I was willing to change this pattern, but I needed a replacement for the things I was so used to saying, something more powerful than these words of strife and criticism.

I found that alternative in Ephesians 5:3-4. *"But fornication,*

7

*and all uncleanness, or covetousness, let it not be once named among you, as becometh saints; Neither filthiness, nor foolish talking, nor jesting, which are not convenient: but rather giving of thanks."* The alternative to speaking ugly is thanksgiving. *The New English Bible* says it this way, *"No coarse, stupid, or flippant talk; these things are out of place; you should rather be thanking God."* I realized that I couldn't speak harshly and thank God simultaneously. I couldn't criticize those around me if I had a thankful attitude about them.

I immediately decided to put this principle to work in my life. Rushing into my son's room one day ready to lambaste him about something he had done, I recognized my old behavior pattern. I just stopped and said to myself, *The Word says that this kind of behavior is out of place,*

*so I am going to stop and thank God.*
I wasn't nearly as angry after I spent
a few minutes praising and thanking
the Lord for him.

We're not supposed to correct our
children in anger. Ephesians 6:4 says,
*"Fathers, do not irritate and provoke
your children to anger—do not exas-
perate them to resentment—but rear
them [tenderly] in the training and discipline and the counsel and admoni-
tion of the Lord" (The Amplified Bible).*
And verse 1 of Chapter 5 said that
we are to *"be...followers of God, as dear
children."* In other words, we are
to imitate God as children imitate
their parents.

When we miss the mark, God
doesn't hit us with a barrage of verbal
abuse! Rather, He corrects us with
gentle reproof, and that's the way
we're to correct our children. When
we're angry, if we'll just stop for a few

minutes and thank the Lord, it will change the way we discipline them.

This approach will work in *any* situation where there's a temptation to tear into someone with cruel and unkind words. When someone crosses you on the job, at school, or wherever, instead of the verbal abuse, let your mouth be filled with praise to your God. He is worthy of your praise! If you are thinking about how good God is, you can't be talking about how bad others are!

A lot of believers don't realize it, but this is what Jesus meant when He said that we are to take up our cross and follow Him. People have some strange ideas about what their cross in life is. Some think it's sickness. Others believe it's poverty. Still others think that their unruly teenagers are their cross to bear. But the one thing that you will never be rid of in this life—the one thing that will be your cross to bear—is unkind, hard-to-love people. There will always be someone who will try to provoke you. But in order to stop strife, you'll have to take up the cross and follow Jesus.

How did Jesus respond to unlovely people? He imitated His heavenly Father and spoke the Word of God. He said, "The words I speak are not My own. I only say what the Father tells Me to say" (see John 8:28). And John 3:34 tells us that because He only spoke the Word of God, He had the Spirit in an unlimited measure. The power of God was Jesus' vindication in every situation, not His smart-aleck words! He didn't use any flippant words. He only said what the Father told Him to say.

In Ephesians 4:29-32, we find the kinds of things the Father is telling *us* to say.

11

**Let no corrupt communication proceed out of your mouth, but that which is good to the use of edifying, that it may minister grace unto the hearers. And grieve not the holy Spirit of God, whereby ye are sealed unto the day of redemption. Let all bitterness, and wrath, and anger, and clamour, and evil speaking, be put away from you, with all malice: And be ye kind one to another, tenderhearted, forgiving one another, even as God for Christ's sake hath forgiven you.**

Notice the words *even as*. We are supposed to be imitating God no matter what the circumstances are. We are supposed to be acting like God, speaking His words and doing His work.

If we keep ourselves busy doing His thing, we won't have time to do *our* thing! We will be so full of God's love that there won't be any room for strife. That's the key to having the power of God manifested in our lives just as it was manifested in Jesus' life.

Smith Wigglesworth is an excellent example. He went into the ministry because he became so involved in the work of God that he just didn't have time to be a plumber anymore. He was so full of the Spirit and so busy preaching to folks one-on-one that he had to go into full-time ministry.

Mr. Wigglesworth jumped onto a fellow's wagon one day and said, "I'm going to stay here until you let me tell you about Jesus." Just to get rid of him, the fellow said, "Well, go ahead and tell me. Then get off my wagon!"

So Mr. Wigglesworth started telling him about how God loved him and wasn't holding his sins against him. After a while, tears started flowing from the fellow's eyes and he said, "Pray for me, Mr. Wigglesworth. I want to accept the Lord." The man died two weeks later. What would have happened to him if someone had not been doing God's work?

That was God's love in action. Men in themselves are not capable of that sincere concern for total strangers. It takes God's love to reach out to others.

God's love must be in your heart in abundance for it to come out of your mouth the way it came out of Smith Wigglesworth, and the best way to be filled with the love of God is to renew your mind to that love.

The way that I renew my mind to the love of God is to study and meditate 1 Corinthians 13:4-8. I read it in the first person like this: "I suffer long and am kind; I do not envy; I do not parade myself; I am not puffed up; I do not behave rudely; I do not seek my own way; I am not provoked; I think no evil; I do not rejoice in iniquity, but I rejoice in the truth; I bear all things; I believe all things; I hope all things, and I endure all things. I never fail." This is a valid confession because God is love, and I am born of God. Therefore, I am born of love.

The love of God in your heart and the praise of God on your lips are an unbeatable team. When an unlovely person tries to provoke you into strife, you will remember, *I am not provoked*. Instead of retaliating, let the praise of God come out of your mouth.

This doesn't mean that you have to let them take advantage of you.

Praise brings the presence of God on the scene and causes some astounding things to happen in the spirit realm. Notice Psalm 8:2. *"Out of the mouth of babes and sucklings hast thou ordained strength because of thine enemies, that thou mightest still the enemy and the avenger."* When Jesus quoted this verse in Matthew 21:16, He said, *"Out of the mouth of babes and sucklings thou hast perfected praise."* Jesus equated praise with strength. Strength against what? Strength against Satan, our only real enemy. Praise stops the devil.

Now look at Psalm 9:2-4. *"I will be glad and rejoice in thee: I will sing praise to thy name, O thou most High. When mine enemies are turned back, they shall fall and perish at thy presence. For thou hast maintained my right and my cause; thou satest in the throne judging right."*

Praise stills the enemy. It stops strife because it stops the source of it—Satan. Praise and love pack a powerful one-two punch. Praise will cause the devil to fall back and perish at the very presence of God coming into a situation, and love never fails. That's why the love of God in your heart and the praise of God on your lips are an unbeatable team. You have not only taken a defensive action against strife, but an offensive action as well!

An excellent example of how praise backs Satan down comes from Aimee Semple McPherson's ministry. She was holding a large tent meeting when some of the townspeople decided to throw kerosene on the tent and "burn that bunch of religious fanatics out of town." They were making so much noise outside the tent that no one could hear the preaching. Aimee McPherson took control of the situation by praising God.

The Lord opened Aimee's eyes to see into the spirit. She noticed that every time she said, "Praise God," the evil spirits that were driving those men cowered and backed away. The men eventually calmed down and became convicted of their wrongdoing. Before the meeting was over, more than half of them gave their lives to the Lord. Not only was the meeting saved, but the men were too!

When you praise God in the midst of strife instead of retaliating, God will not only maintain *your* right and *your* cause, He will maintain the right and cause of the other person as well. Because He is no respecter of persons, God will show you a way to have a no-lose situation. Everyone will win because Satan will lose!

Beginning today, you can conquer strife. Make a decision to keep yourself full of the love of God. Meditate the "love chapter" (1 Corinthians 13:4-8). Confess it in the first person several times a day. And when others provoke you, don't retaliate. Instead, give thanks to God for His goodness and watch His presence come on the scene and put strife under your feet where it belongs!

## Prayer for Salvation and Baptism in the Holy Spirit

Heavenly Father, I come to You in the Name of Jesus. Your Word says, *"Whosoever shall call on the name of the Lord shall be saved"* (Acts 2:21). I am calling on You. I pray and ask Jesus to come into my heart and be Lord over my life according to Romans 10:9-10. *"If thou shalt confess with thy mouth the Lord Jesus, and shalt believe in thine heart that God hath raised him from the dead, thou shalt be saved."* I do that now. I confess that Jesus is Lord, and I believe in my heart that God raised Him from the dead.

I am now reborn! I am a Christian— a child of Almighty God! I am saved! You also said in Your Word, *"If ye then, being evil, know how to give good gifts unto your children: HOW MUCH MORE shall your heavenly Father give the Holy Spirit to them that ask him?"* (Luke 11:13). I'm also asking You to fill me with the Holy Spirit.

Holy Spirit, rise up within me as I praise God. I fully expect to speak with other tongues as You give me the utterance (Acts 2:4).

Begin to praise God for filling you with the Holy Spirit. Speak those words and syllables you receive—not in your own language, but the language given to you by the Holy Spirit. You have to use your own voice. God will not force you to speak. Worship and praise Him in your heavenly language—in other tongues.

Continue with the blessing God has given you and pray in tongues each day.

You are a born-again, Spirit-filled believer. You'll never be the same!

Find a good Word of God preaching church, and become a part of a church family who will love and care for you as you love and care for them.

We need to be hooked up to each other. It increases our strength in God. It's God's plan for us.

# About the Author

Kenneth Copeland is co-founder and preside of Kenneth Copeland Ministries in Fort Wort Texas, and best-selling author of books th include *Managing God's Mutual Funds, How Discipline Your Flesh* and *Honor—Walking Honesty, Truth and Integrity.*

Now in his 30th year as minister of the gospel Christ and teacher of God's Word, Kenneth is t recording artist of such award-winning albums his Grammy nominated *Only the Redeemed, In F Presence, He Is Jehovah* and his most recen released *What a God You Are.* He also co-stars the character Wichita Slim in the children's adve ture videos *The Gunslinger, Covenant Rider* and t movie *The Treasure of Eagle Mountain,* and Daniel Lyon in the Commander Kellie and t Superkids_SM video *Armor of Light.*

With the help of offices and staff in t United States, Canada, England, Austral South Africa and Ukraine, Kenneth is fulfilling l vision to boldly preach the uncompromised Wo of God from the top of this world, to the botto and all the way around. His ministry reach millions of people worldwide through daily an weekly TV broadcasts, magazines, audio and vid teaching tapes, conventions and campaigns.

# Other Books Available From
# Kenneth Copeland

Available in Spanish

# World Offices
# of Kenneth Copeland Ministries

For more information about KCM and a
catalog, please write the office nearest you:

Kenneth Copeland Ministries
Fort Worth, Texas  76192-0001

Kenneth Copeland
Locked Bag 2600
Mansfield Delivery Centre
QUEENSLAND 4122
AUSTRALIA

Kenneth Copela
Post Office Box 1
BATH
BA1 1GD
ENGLAND

Kenneth Copeland
Private Bag X 909
FOUNTAINEBLEAU
2032
REPUBLIC OF SOUTH AFRICA

Kenneth Copelar
Post Office Box 3
Surrey
BRITISH COLUM
V3T 5B6
CANADA

220123 MINSK
REPUBLIC OF BELARUS
Post Office 123
P/B 35
Kenneth Copeland Ministries